Better Sleep at Last?

Better Sleep at Last?

Helping Adults Switch Off and Relax For Sleep.

A.C French.

Copyright Information

ISBN: 979-8-3037-8872-5
First Edition.
Copyright © 2024 A.C French. All Rights Reserved.

No part of this publication may be reproduced, distributed, or transmitted in any form or by any means, including photocopying, recording, or other electronic or mechanical methods, without the prior written permission of the author, except in the case of brief quotations embodied in critical reviews and certain other non-commercial uses permitted by US copyright law.
For permission requests, contact the author, A.C French at contactacfrench @gmail.com

Disclaimer

No responsibility or liability is accepted by the author, A.C French for any situation arising from, or connected to any use made of this book. The contents of this book are for entertainment purposes only. The author is providing this book and its contents on an "as is" basis and makes no representations or warranties of any kind with respect to this book or its contents. *The use of this book implies your acceptance of this disclaimer.*

Preface

Better Sleep at Last? is a book that might very easily have remained unpublished if it was not for the support and encouragement of my wife, Young Joo. Young Joo being someone able to sleep within a minute of her head hitting the pillow. Perhaps, better still, she would sleep through an earthquake, *I am guessing,* though actually that is probably not ideal, nonetheless the point is made. I, on the other hand, have struggled, both to fall asleep and to get back to sleep after waking up during the night.

After simply accepting the situation, and doing the best I could, *nothing*, I decided that I needed something to change. Perhaps this is because as I get older I am generally less tolerant of things that affect my or better *our* quality of life.

No matter the underlying reason, the book is now here and I am now much happier as a result. Not just because the book is finished, but because in the course of writing the quality of my sleep has improved. I have to say too that I feel less liable to get stressed over things generally, so a definite plus for my relationship with my wife.

Testing in real time, the ideas contained in the book against my personal experiences of being unable to get to sleep, has been a great help in shaping the book's final format. Thank you for the opportunity to share this book with you; I hope it helps *you* to more easily switch off, relax and enjoy improved sleep.

Acknowledgements

Thank you to my wife Young Joo for all your patience, support, and encouragement. *Better Sleep at Last?* would never have happened without you.

Contents

<u>Chapter</u>   <u>Pg.</u>

1. Introduction 1
2. Scope of this Book 3
3. Breathing 5
4. Relaxing Body and Mind 7
5. Setting Expectations.. 9
6. The Plan 11
7. Relaxation Routines 13
8. About the Visualizations 17
9. The Visualizations 19- 40

    Adds up to Ten
    Eye Eye
    One Strange Ball
    Positive Vibes
    Stepping Up
    Count 3 3 2
    Finger Linking Good
    Heavy Eyes
    Thumb Pressure
    A Fluid Situation
    Waves Becoming Lighter
    Heading to Sleep
    Six Golden Fields
    Thumbs and Fingers
    TV Shapes
    Comfy Cloud
    Green Dreams
    Mixing it Up
    Merry-go-round
    Feet in the Water

Chapter	Pg.
9. The Visualizations (Cont.)..................	41- 66

    Tennis ball Time
    Light Source
    Red Card, Blue Card
    On the Tilt
    Music Starts and Stops
    Icy Table
    Snowy Hill
    Watch the Birdie
    Long Run
    Colored Cars
    Bus in Motion
    Spell It Out
    Deeper.. Deeper
    Folding Paper
    Pencil Circles
    All Fingers and Thumbs
    Platforms and Ladders
    Bright Lights and Shades
    Light Sleep
    Cloud Jumping
    Tumbling Jeans
    Bowled Over
    Stay On Course
    Calmer View
    Polished to a Shine
    Blowing in the Wind

Other Considerations for Better Sleep	67
About the Author	68
Useful Sources of Information	69

1. Introduction

Better Sleep at Last? came into being as a result of frequent nights spent just laying in bed, simply unable to sleep. Insomnia wasn't something just other people suffered from.

One night; I remember quite clearly just lying there as usual, thinking about how there must be a way to fall asleep more easily. Yet, the more I thought things through, the more awake I became. So I tried something; just focusing on the word *sleep* itself and adding positive words in front of it. This simple act, of just thinking about positive words that I could add in front of the word sleep, delivered results. Results, that is, in the form of waking up in the morning and realizing that *I had just had a good night's sleep.*

I tried to work back through my thoughts from the night before to see if I could remember the last thing that had been on my mind while lying there awake. I was able to remember that I had added positive words such as nice, good, relaxing, essential, for instance, in front of the word sleep and repeated the same to myself in my mind as I had lain there.

The fact that it was at that point *morning*, told me that what I had done in terms of repeating the specific words to myself the night before had sent me off to sleep.
To hopefully see if I could prove my point, I did the same again the night after; it worked again.

I enjoyed a sense of relief, in that something I had done had actually made a difference. This, despite the fact that it was just an initial experiment. Nonetheless, I resolved to use it often.

This early success led me to try to find other simple thoughts or visualizations that I could test and use as a back up in effect. In itself this became helpful in getting off to sleep, i.e just the idea of trying to find new ways to train my mind to drop off to sleep, seemed to work too.

I decided to test out more and more ideas, especially in regard to linking visualization of certain images or actions with slower, controlled breathing. I found this made a big difference both in terms of how relaxed I became, and also how I was able to better concentrate on the actions in a visualization, because they were tied to a breathing pattern.

I soon felt ready to start compiling a short list of a few favorites that I knew would definitely work for me.
So that's really the bones of how the book came together. It started out as a few ideas to help me personally fine tune ways I could more easily fall asleep but then led me on to think about how my ideas may also help others who experience problems getting to sleep.

I like to think that something I did, potentially made someone else's life a little easier or better in some small way.

2. Scope of this Book

There can be many reasons for adult sleep problems and insomnia, *the state of being unable to get to sleep or stay asleep.* Insomnia also presents itself in different forms and with different levels of severity.

Health issues, lifestyle, habits, life events, concerns about family and relationships, work, finances and more, can play a big part in the condition. For some, the insomnia they suffer from is not linked to other health conditions or problems.

The scope of this book however, is limited to sharing a range of visualizations, breathing and relaxation routines, as part of a process, ultimately designed to offer you a better chance of just drifting off to sleep.

Whilst this book should help those with trouble getting to sleep, sleep onset insomnia; or those with difficulties getting back to sleep after waking, sleep maintenance insomnia, the book is not offering science based advice and guidance on how to overcome insomnia or any type of sleep disorder.

3. <u>Breathing</u>

Throughout the book you'll find mention of *long, deep breathing*. As will become apparent, this is a central aspect of both the relaxation routines and visualizations themselves.

While using this book, it is recommended that you try to breathe *in* slowly <u>through the nose</u> and then *exhale* slowly also <u>through the nose.</u>

That said, if exhaling through the nose proves uncomfortable or overly labored, breathe out through the mouth instead. The aim is that you are able to breathe easily yet in a controlled manner.

<u>Note.</u>
In the event that there are reasons, medical or otherwise, why nasal breathing is uncomfortable or indeed not possible, again, please instead breathe via the mouth.

It should also be noted that in rare circumstances, the act of focusing on controlling one's breathing can induce a panic response; in which case continued use of the book is not recommended.

4. <u>Relaxing Body and Mind.</u>

Following experimentation with synchronizing *deeper* breathing, to certain actions within a visualization, I also thought more about how I could better prepare my body prior to actually beginning a visualization.

I used a short easy to remember *Body Relaxation routine*, that I could perform while laying in bed. Nothing too complicated and involved.

Additionally, as a result of often being unable to switch off from concerns or even just general thoughts playing on my mind, I tried out a few short mind calming routines; before finding one that was both effective and easy to perform.

This allowed me on most occasions, to *pause* thoughts that might otherwise prevent my mind from being as receptive as it could be to the visualizations. This is something that whilst initially challenging, definitely became easier with practice.

These short routines are outlined in the chapter on Relaxation Routines.

5. Setting Expectations.

Let's first set some expectations: There are no guarantees that the visualizations and relaxation routines in this book will *definitely* help you get to sleep. It can be expected, however, that the act of performing the *process* outlined in the book, should, over time, make it easier for you to fall asleep. This is because in large part, the book is conditioning the mind to *switch off* and *prepare for sleep.*

This is helped by the fact that deep breathing routines are linked to certain actions within the visualizations. The focus this requires, means that the mind is less likely to be distracted by other thoughts. Also important in this regard, is the repetitive structure found at the start and end of each visualization.

So whilst the actual visualizations are different, the *positive suggestions* being made to the mind remain constant. I.e., the feeling of sinking into the bed, or telling ourselves how what we are about to do will help us get to sleep more easily, for instance.

While sleep may *just happen,* it very well also may not. Equally, sleep may come quickly or it may take time. So think of the book as a kind of *support system* that you can call on to try something new; rather than just laying there wishing you could get to sleep.

6. The Plan.

Ideally, first allow some time to get used to the relaxation routines. This is because in addition to remembering how to perform these routines, you will also need to remember the actual visualization itself.

<u>So for the first three days:</u>

After going to bed, perform only the body relaxation and mind calming routines. This will hopefully mean that by the time you start on a visualization, your mind will be more receptive and more able to concentrate.

<u>After the initial three days:</u>

Carry out the Body Relaxation and Mind Calming routines as before, then begin with visualization one. If you fall asleep, i.e if the first visualization works, use <u>that visualization</u> again on any subsequent night that you cannot sleep.

So, basically, if it works, stick with it, until such a time as it doesn't. At which point move to the next.

<u>If you don't fall asleep</u>

If you don't fall asleep, firstly don't worry, and as importantly <u>don't</u> move on to visualization two on the same night. Simply tell yourself that you'll try the next visualization tomorrow, and focus instead on just slowing your breathing and relaxing as best you can.

If you wake up but find it hard to get back to sleep

First use the Mind Calming routine; then try to recall and perform the visualization you *last* used to get to sleep, or used to try to get to sleep. Make sure you are comfortable in the bed, continue with long, slow breathing and tell yourself that *just relaxing more* is okay. Don't *try too hard* to sleep or you can be sure it will never happen!

As you go forward, try to think of the book, not as some kind of magical fix, but a process you can follow that might help; hopefully you will eventually find a visualization that works for you. As mentioned, the repetitive nature of the process itself should help overtime. Try to accept that it is okay to not be in *full on* sleep and that if you have relaxed your body and mind and slowed your breathing, you are already further along, than if you had just laid there stressing out.

So in effect, all is not lost just because you are not deep in sleep. This, ironically, could help improve your state of relaxation to the point where sleep follows anyway.

7. Relaxation Routines

Use both of these routines prior to each visualization. The routines are purposely very short, but of course feel free to adapt them in any way you wish.

Body Relaxation. (One minute)

Close your eyes, and use the index finger and thumb of one hand at the same time to gently circle and massage around the outside of both eye sockets.

Circle your shoulders four times high against the side of your neck, before moving your head left to right, trying to almost touch your ear on to your shoulder, alternating twice on each side.

Shake your hands loosely side to side from your wrists for a short time. Then spread your hands and extend your fingers, before clenching your hands into tight fists, repeat this four times.

Slowly circle your ankles around, first with an in to out motion, then reverse.

Lastly, repeat the index finger and thumb eyes massage again.

After you have performed the Body Relaxation routine, feel free to change your position and get more comfortable in the bed.

Mind Calming (Two minutes)

To be performed directly after body relaxation. Remember to use nasal breathing, both in and out.

<u>Keep your eyes closed.</u> Take five long, slow deep breaths. Concentrate on starting and ending the breath very smoothly. Allow a two second pause between each breath.

<u>Then, continuing to breathe deeply,</u> imagine your bed slowly raising up, with you on it. Lifting off the ground, until it is high above any thoughts or worries that may be on your mind. After a short while, imagine yourself looking around, and noticing that all you can see are a few clouds, in an otherwise blue sky.

As you continue to breathe deeply, see yourself relaxing back on your bed in the sky, enjoying the feeling of being separated from everything below, especially what may have been on your mind before. Allow a feeling of calm and wellbeing to build; enjoy it and tell yourself it is well deserved. Continue to breathe slowly and deeply.

Two minutes by the way, shakes out at around twelve slow full deep breaths. There is no rush to complete the Mind Calming routine; the two minutes is for guidance only, take more time if you prefer.

Note on Mind Calming routine

As previously mentioned, outside of health problems, the unfortunate truth about most forms of insomnia is that it is often the result of worries or thoughts surrounding the events and realities of everyday life.

Obviously, the book does not aim to gloss over the potential importance of such realities or concerns. However, the Mind Calming routine *is designed* to provide a short time and space, *and also reason* where it is okay not to have a worry or thought top of mind at bedtime.

Finally, it should be noted, in the event that you are trying to get back to sleep after waking up during the night, it is likely that the Mind Calming routine <u>alone</u> will be sufficient, prior to the visualization stage.

8. About the Visualizations.

Before trying to use a visualization, you should try to remember the key idea and the breathing pattern involved. Ideally, make sure you can picture the whole visualization that you intend to use, from start to finish, before laying down on the bed; you will need to recall it directly after completing the relaxation routines.

More on the visualizations:

- Each visualization includes an action that is linked to a deep breathing pattern. This is to help make it easier to sustain focus during the visualization; leaving less room for distracting thoughts.

- Some visualizations or images may seem a little strange, this is because they have to be both memorable and easy to visualize.

- Every visualization starts and ends in the same way, because you are conditioning your mind to follow the same routine, so the whole *process* becomes more natural and easier to remember and perform.

- It is unlikely that you will be able to easily relate to every visualization in the book, but that's ok, some will work better for some people than others.

- When you find a visualization that *does work* for you, stick with that one going forward. If it subsequently fails to work of course, there are plenty more in the book to try.

- The idea is not to try to use lots of different visualizations to help you sleep, but instead just to find one that works for you.

- Each visualization has an easy to remember name.

- Certain visualizations also have a physical component, such as for instance, *tensing and releasing fists,* or *lifting and lowering the head*. Feel free to use these physical actions as part of other visualizations too, should you wish to get creative.

- There are no fixed rules of course, although you will need to tie these actions into the breathing pattern used in a particular visualization.

9. The Visualizations.

If you find some of the visualizations challenging to begin with, try to remember the more you practice, the easier it will become.

The goal is not to be perfect, but simply to allow the visualization to give you a focal point for your thoughts. Remember, you have a great many visualizations to try should you need to, and as you get more used to focusing on and controlling your breathing pattern, you will hopefully find relaxation and sleep come more quickly.

Adds up to Ten

After performing both relaxation routines:
Keep your eyes closed, tell yourself that what you are about to do is going to help you get ready to sleep. Take three further long deep breaths, as you try to feel yourself sinking into the bed.

In your mind, slowly count *one* and *nine* (adds up to ten) then after a slow deep breath count *two* and *eight*; continue with *three* and *seven*, *four* and *six* and so on until you reach *nine* and *one* (taking a long deep breath between each count. Then repeat, again starting with *one* and *nine*, *two* and *eight* etc as before. Continue this process three or four times, once more breathing deeply between each count.

After a while, tell yourself that because of what you are doing or just did, you are now ready to just drift off into sleep.
Feel that with each breath, you are becoming more tired and sinking further into the bed.

Positive Vibes

After performing both relaxation routines:
Keep your eyes closed, tell yourself that what you are about to do is going to help you get ready to sleep. Take three further long deep breaths, as you try to feel yourself sinking into the bed.

Then, think of the word *sleep*; say it over in your mind three or four times. You are then going to add the word *good* in front of the word sleep and then slowly say the phrase *good sleep* slowly three times to yourself, taking a long deep breath each time. Continue this process but change the phrase to *perfect sleep*, again breathing slowly each time you say the phrase in your head.

From this point feel free to choose your own positive words to add to create new phrases, such as *fine, quiet, peaceful, needed, great, relaxing, enjoyable, nice, brilliant* for instance. Any word is okay as long as it creates a positive phrase. Continue the breathing pattern as you go. If you can't think of new words to add just repeat some of those you previously thought of.

After a while, tell yourself that because of what you are doing or just did, you are now ready to just drift off into sleep. Feel that with each breath, you are becoming more tired and sinking further into the bed.

Eye Eye

After performing both relaxation routines:
Keep your eyes closed, tell yourself that what you are about to do is going to help you get ready to sleep. Take three further long deep breaths, as you try to feel yourself sinking into the bed.

As in the Body Relaxation routine, using the thumb and ring finger of one hand, gently massage the area all around both eye sockets. Be careful not to push on the skin directly over the eye. As you do this, take long, deep breaths. After a couple of minutes, lower your hand and stop the massage.

Continue to breathe deeply and then just *imagine* you are still performing the massage like before (i.e without actually using your hand). Repeat the above once more, before ceasing the massage altogether. From this point just concentrate on slowing your breathing, while thinking about how relaxing the eye massage was.

After a while, tell yourself that because of what you are doing or just did, you are now ready to just drift off into sleep. Feel that with each breath, you are becoming more tired and sinking further into the bed.

One Strange Ball

After performing both relaxation routines:
Keep your eyes closed, tell yourself that what you are about to do is going to help you get ready to sleep. Take three further long deep breaths, as you try to feel yourself sinking into the bed.

Then see yourself standing comfortably holding a basketball at chest height .This is no ordinary ball. If you try to bounce it, you can't, it just remains in your hands.

You work out that if you push down on the ball it will eventually reach the floor. Once it does, it wants to pop back up again fast. So in order to control it, you have to push against the top of the ball again as it rises.

Once the ball is back up to chest height, the pressure you are applying forces the ball slowly back down to the floor, and so the cycle repeats.

As you push the ball down to the floor you take two long deep breaths in and out; so the ball reaches the floor at the end of the second breath. As the ball rises again, you take two more long deep breaths before the ball is back to chest height again and you begin the next push downwards. Repeat and continue for a few minutes.

After a while, tell yourself that because of what you are doing or just did, you are now ready to just drift off into sleep.
Feel that with each breath, you are becoming more tired and sinking further into the bed.

Stepping Up

After performing both relaxation routines:
Keep your eyes closed, tell yourself that what you are about to do is going to help you get ready to sleep. Take three further long deep breaths, as you try to feel yourself sinking into the bed.

You are about to walk up the steps of an apartment building because the elevators are out of action. You live on the ninth floor. You begin to climb steadily upwards. The pace you set to reach each new floor, corresponds to the time it takes to complete four long, deep breaths.

So, two long deep breaths to the halfway point, before turning to climb the remaining stairway to the next floor each time. Once you reach each new floor, you take two further long, deep breaths before continuing up.

If, by the way, you fail to reach your floor and feel too tired at any point, just see yourself sitting and resting or falling asleep where you are on the stairs.

After a while, tell yourself that because of what you are doing or just did, you are now ready to just drift off into sleep.
Feel that with each breath, you are becoming more tired and sinking further into the bed.

Dark Patches

After performing both relaxation routines:
Keep your eyes closed, tell yourself that what you are about to do is going to help you get ready to sleep. Take three further long deep breaths, as you try to feel yourself sinking into the bed.

Through closed eyes, you become aware of dark patches moving around. Try to focus on those dark patches and when you see brighter flashes or brighter patches try to ignore them, instead just focus on the dark patches.

As you do this, continue to breathe deeply and tell yourself that by focusing on the darker patches the brighter patches or flashes will become less noticable. This indeed seems to happen as you continue to take long, deep breaths.

Imagine, that in some way, your actual breathing is helping to filter out the bigger flashes or brighter patches. So feel that as you breathe in, you are also breathing in the flashes or brighter patches, cleaning the view as it were. This leads to a growing sense of calm.

After a while, tell yourself that because of what you are doing or just did, you are now ready to just drift off into sleep.
Feel that with each breath, you are becoming more tired and sinking further into the bed.

Count 3 3 2

After performing both relaxation routines:
Keep your eyes closed, tell yourself that what you are about to do is going to help you get ready to sleep. Take three further long deep breaths, as you try to feel yourself sinking into the bed.

Now imagine that the mattress below you is one of the most comfortable mattresses ever made. Feel that it supports your body perfectly as you relax. Then begin to count to three as you breathe in slowly. Don't rush, try to make sure that you reach the count of three just as you have finished breathing in.

Then count to three again as you slowly breathe out; try to make sure that you reach the count of three just as you have finished slowly breathing out. Then before taking your next deep breath in, *slowly count to two.* Repeat and continue, trying to focus on the three, three, two count breathing pattern.

After a while, tell yourself that because of what you are doing or just did, you are now ready to just drift off into sleep.
Feel that with each breath, you are becoming more tired and sinking further into the bed.

Finger Linking Good

After performing both relaxation routines:
Keep your eyes closed, tell yourself that what you are about to do is going to help you get ready to sleep. Take three further long deep breaths, as you try to feel yourself sinking into the bed.

Lay back on the bed and place the palms of your hands together. Allow your fingers to drop, linking the fingers of each hand together. Keeping your fingers locked try to pull your hands apart, but don't actually allow the hands to separate. This should create tension in your upper arms and back. Hold this tensed position for three long deep breaths, then relax.

After three more long deep breaths repeat the process <u>twice more</u>, then allow your hands to separate and relax. Continue the deep breathing and imagine any tension that you felt has now left your body.

After a while, tell yourself that because of what you are doing or just did, you are now ready to just drift off into sleep. Feel that with each breath, you are becoming more tired and sinking further into the bed.

Heavy Eyes

After performing both relaxation routines:
Keep your eyes closed, tell yourself that what you are about to do is going to help you get ready to sleep. Take three further long deep breaths, as you try to feel yourself sinking into the bed.

Then, see yourself sitting in a comfortable armchair. As you sit in the chair you feel yourself sinking down into the comfortable cushions. You take another big deep breath, hold it and then release. You continue to do this as you sit in the chair. You imagine that you want to open your eyes, but they seem too heavy.

Instead, you focus on your breathing, in and out, telling yourself that the feeling of having heavy eyes is good. You become more and more relaxed and continue to breathe deeply, happy with the fact that it seems hard to open your eyes.

After a while, tell yourself that because of what you are doing or just did, you are now ready to just drift off into sleep.
Feel that with each breath, you are becoming more tired and sinking further into the bed.

Thumb Pressure

After performing both relaxation routines:
Keep your eyes closed, tell yourself that what you are about to do is going to help you get ready to sleep. Take three further long deep breaths, as you try to feel yourself sinking into the bed.

Now place your left thumb on top of your left index finger and gently press down and hold. As you do this take a long deep breath, then move your thumb to the next finger and repeat. Continue this process, ensuring to follow the same deep breathing pattern ,until you finish on the little finger.

Then switch to the right hand and repeat as before. Once you have completed each hand, finally repeat for both hands at the same time. At this point just relax your hands and try to focus on slowing your breathing as much as possible.

After a while, tell yourself that because of what you are doing or just did, you are now ready to just drift off into sleep.
Feel that with each breath, you are becoming more tired and sinking further into the bed.

A Fluid Situation

After performing both relaxation routines:
Keep your eyes closed, tell yourself that what you are about to do is going to help you get ready to sleep. Take three further long deep breaths, as you try to feel yourself sinking into the bed.

Then, as your eyes rest you start to see primarily dark yet also lighter shapes or spaces floating and mixing into one another. Imagine you are looking at the surface of a fluid, on which the darker shades are in constant motion, often slowly growing and melding into one another.

Concentrate on your breathing as you do this, with long breaths in and out. After four or five breaths, try to imagine that the fluid has a mind calming quality, and that watching helps you relax.

Tell yourself that this feeling of relaxation increases every four or five breaths. As you continue by the way, there is no need to strain as you try to perform this visualization, instead try to allow all tension to leave the eyes.

After a while, tell yourself that because of what you are doing or just did, you are now ready to just drift off into sleep. Feel that with each breath, you are becoming more tired and sinking further into the bed.

Waves Becoming Lighter

After performing both relaxation routines:
Keep your eyes closed, tell yourself that what you are about to do is going to help you get ready to sleep. Take three further long deep breaths, as you try to feel yourself sinking into the bed.

Then see yourself sitting on the sand under a palm tree on the beach. In the distance you can hear the waves gently lapping against the shore. You notice that the waves are in time with your breathing; your breathing is slow and deep.

As you breathe in the wave comes in, as you breathe out the wave goes out; you feel at peace and very relaxed. Your breathing continues to slow and you try to count the waves in sets of three. With each set the waves become a little lighter.

After a while, tell yourself that because of what you are doing or just did, you are now ready to just drift off into sleep.
Feel that with each breath, you are becoming more tired and sinking further into the bed.

Heading to Sleep

After performing both relaxation routines:
Keep your eyes closed, tell yourself that what you are about to do is going to help you get ready to sleep. Take three further long deep breaths, as you try to feel yourself sinking into the bed.

Now gently push your head down into the pillow and lightly hold it there, for a count of three long deep breaths, then relax. Next, turn onto your left side and raise your head a little off the pillow; again hold this position for three long deep breaths, before relaxing once more. Now turn onto your right side and repeat the process, again with the three long breaths.

After this, return to your original position on your back. At this point simply <u>imagine you are performing the routine above again.</u> Be sure to continue the deep breathing pattern as you do so.

After a while, tell yourself that because of what you are doing or just did, you are now ready to just drift off into sleep. Feel that with each breath, you are becoming more tired and sinking further into the bed.

Six Golden Fields

After performing both relaxation routines:
Keep your eyes closed, tell yourself that what you are about to do is going to help you get ready to sleep. Take three further long deep breaths, as you try to feel yourself sinking into the bed.

Then, imagine you're floating high in the sky. You look down and you see six golden fields of corn bathed in sunshine far below you. Then you notice cloud shadow slowly start to cover each of the fields one by one. This happens in time with your breathing; long, deep, slow breaths.

So each time you breathe in you see another field covered by shadow. Once all fields have been covered by shadow, rest for three more long deep breaths, and then repeat.

After a while, tell yourself that because of what you are doing or just did, you are now ready to just drift off into sleep.
Feel that with each breath, you are becoming more tired and sinking further into the bed.

Clench and Extend

After performing both relaxation routines:
Keep your eyes closed, tell yourself that what you are about to do is going to help you get ready to sleep. Take three further long deep breaths, as you try to feel yourself sinking into the bed.

As you lay there, stretch out your left arm. Try to bend your wrist backwards as you open your palm and fingers. As you hold that position, take three long deep breaths and then slowly relax and lower your arm.

After three more deep breaths, repeat this for your right arm. Again take the three long deep breaths while you hold the position. Continue this process, with the left and right arm; repeat several times.

After a while, tell yourself that because of what you are doing or just did, you are now ready to just drift off into sleep. Feel that with each breath, you are becoming more tired and sinking further into the bed.

Thumbs and Fingers

After performing both relaxation routines:
Keep your eyes closed, tell yourself that what you are about to do is going to help you get ready to sleep. Take three further long deep breaths, as you try to feel yourself sinking into the bed.

Then, slowly touch and hold the index finger of each hand with the thumb, making a circle. Next, after every two new long, deep breaths, switch the thumbs to the adjacent finger and hold there.

After two further long, deep breaths, switch the thumbs back to the index finger again. Repeat this switching process, after every two breaths. If you can, try to use a little less pressure between your finger and thumb each time.

After a while, tell yourself that because of what you are doing or just did, you are now ready to just drift off into sleep. Feel that with each breath, you are becoming more tired and sinking further into the bed.

TV Shapes

After performing both relaxation routines:
Keep your eyes closed, tell yourself that what you are about to do is going to help you get ready to sleep. Take three further long deep breaths, as you try to feel yourself sinking into the bed.

Then imagine you're looking at a dark TV screen with a large white circle in the middle of it. You focus on the circle as you continue to breathe deeply. After three or four more breaths you see a large white square has replaced the circle on the TV screen. Again you stare at the image while continuing to breathe deeply.

After three or four more breaths a large white triangle appears in place of the square. You focus on the triangle as your breathing slows further. After three or four more breaths begin again with the circle and repeat.

After a while, tell yourself that because of what you are doing or just did, you are now ready to just drift off into sleep.
Feel that with each breath, you are becoming more tired and sinking further into the bed.

Comfy Cloud

After performing both relaxation routines:
Keep your eyes closed, tell yourself that what you are about to do is going to help you get ready to sleep. Take three further long deep breaths, as you try to feel yourself sinking into the bed.

Then, imagine that your comfortable pillow is actually a cloud; a very soft white cloud. The cloud's only purpose is to make you feel as comfortable as possible, to help you sleep. You imagine that other clouds occasionally float by but that yours is the best cloud, it's the most comfortable and soft.

After a little time you notice that your breathing is slowing and you focus on controlling your breathing in and out, as you relax further. Now you notice another cloud floats by after every third long deep breath; this continues.

After a while, tell yourself that because of what you are doing or just did, you are now ready to just drift off into sleep.
Feel that with each breath, you are becoming more tired and sinking further into the bed.

Green Dreams

After performing both relaxation routines:
Keep your eyes closed, tell yourself that what you are about to do is going to help you get ready to sleep. Take three further long deep breaths, as you try to feel yourself sinking into the bed.

Then, think of the color green and how mind calming it can be. Imagine everything in your room is slowly being colored green. In your mind, go from one side of the room, over the floor and furniture.. seeing it all slowly turn green, while continuing to breathe deeply.

Several long deep breaths later, repeat the process of seeing everything in the room slowly turn green. Continue just thinking about the color green and how it is making you more and more relaxed and helping you drift off to sleep.

After a while, tell yourself that because of what you are doing or just did, you are now ready to just drift off into sleep.
Feel that with each breath, you are becoming more tired and sinking further into the bed.

Mixing it Up

After performing both relaxation routines:
Keep your eyes closed, tell yourself that what you are about to do is going to help you get ready to sleep. Take three more long deep breaths, and try to feel that you are sinking into the bed.

Now, imagine that you are holding a can of white paint. You add a little green paint and slowly begin to stir. Do this slowly in time with your breathing. Adding a little more green after every three long deep breaths.

Every time you add a little more green and stir you notice what was once the white paint, becoming greener and greener. Eventually the paint has turned dark green. You continue to gently stir the paint round and round.

After a while, tell yourself that because of what you are doing or just did, you are now ready to just drift off into sleep.
Feel that with each breath, you are becoming more tired and sinking further into the bed.

Merry-go-round

After performing both relaxation routines:
Keep your eyes closed, tell yourself that what you are about to do is going to help you get ready to sleep. Take three further long deep breaths, as you try to feel yourself sinking into the bed.

Then, imagine you are sitting on a thick padded seat, on a merry-go-round that is slowly spinning. Each revolution of the merry-go-round takes the same time as two long deep breaths in and out.

Imagine yourself relaxing back in your seat and over-time feel your breathing slowing a little more. So each revolution begins to take longer. You feel your body is becoming more relaxed and enjoy the slow motion of the merry-go-round as it turns.

After a while, tell yourself that because of what you are doing or just did, you are now ready to just drift off into sleep. Feel that with each breath, you are becoming more tired and sinking further into the bed.

Feet in the Water

After performing both relaxation routines:
Keep your eyes closed, tell yourself that what you are about to do is going to help you get ready to sleep. Take three further long deep breaths, as you try to feel yourself sinking into the bed.

Then, imagine you are walking barefoot on a sandy beach. As you walk, you control your breathing. Long, deep breaths, in and out. You can hear the waves gently slapping against the shore. You decide to sit down; then lie back on the sand, stretching your feet out into the water.

Again, you focus on your breathing, in and out. As this continues, you feel yourself becoming increasingly tired. You enjoy the sensation of the water playing over your feet, every second breath.

After a while, tell yourself that because of what you are doing or just did, you are now ready to just drift off into sleep. Feel that with each breath, you are becoming more tired and sinking further into the bed.

Tennis ball Time

After performing both relaxation routines:
Keep your eyes closed, tell yourself that what you are about to do is going to help you get ready to sleep. Take three further long deep breaths, as you try to feel yourself sinking into the bed.

Imagine you're sitting down on the floor with your back against the wall. After taking a long deep breath, you throw a tennis ball you are holding against the opposite wall nearby. It bounces off the wall, hits the ground before coming back to you.

As the ball hits the wall, count *one,* count *two* as it hits the floor and *three* as you catch it again. Repeat the long deep breath before throwing the ball again, counting one, two, three as you do so. Repeat and continue the deep breathing, throwing and counting each time.

After a while you begin to feel tired so you stop throwing the ball, and see yourself just lying down in front of the wall.

After a while, tell yourself that because of what you are doing or just did, you are now ready to just drift off into sleep. Feel that with each breath, you are becoming more tired and sinking further into the bed.

Light Source

After performing both relaxation routines:
Keep your eyes closed, tell yourself that what you are about to do is going to help you get ready to sleep. Take three further long deep breaths, as you try to feel yourself sinking into the bed.

Then let your eyes *half-open* and gently scan around for any lighter area in the room or an ambient light source. Turn your head, and body if necessary so that you are comfortably facing the brighter part of the room/ light source.

Continue to breathe deeply for a minute or so. Then as you breathe out let your still half-closed eyes, fully close. As you next breathe in, allow your eyes to partly open just a very small amount, enough so that you can see the brighter area/light source again.

Then as you breathe out allow your eyes to relax into the closed position again. Repeat the process above, if you can, over time, opening your eyes even less as you continue.

After a while, tell yourself that because of what you are doing or just did, you are now ready to just drift off into sleep.
Feel that with each breath, you are becoming more tired and sinking further into the bed.

Red Card, Blue Card

After performing both relaxation routines:
Keep your eyes closed, tell yourself that what you are about to do is going to help you get ready to sleep. Take three further long deep breaths, as you try to feel yourself sinking into the bed.

Then, imagine you are sitting at a table. In front of you are two decks of colored cards. One deck is red, the other blue. The objective is to create one new deck using alternate cards taken from the other decks. This is to be done in time with your breathing.

Breathe in as you imagine picking up a red card, then slowly breathe out as you place it down on the table as the first card of the new deck. Repeat this as you take a blue card and lay it on top of the red card. Continue taking alternate cards as your breathing slows further.

After a while, tell yourself that because of what you are doing or just did, you are now ready to just drift off into sleep.
Feel that with each breath, you are becoming more tired and sinking further into the bed.

On the Tilt

After performing both relaxation routines:
Keep your eyes closed, tell yourself that what you are about to do is going to help you get ready to sleep. Take three further long deep breaths, as you try to feel yourself sinking into the bed.

Imagine you can feel the weight of your body sinking into the mattress as you relax. Continue to breathe in and out slowly and as you do, and after a short while imagine that you feel the mattress slowly tilt very slightly to the right. After two more long deep breaths, you imagine the mattress then levels up again.

After a further two long deep breaths imagine the mattress has tilted very slightly to the left. Again it re-centers after two more breaths. This tilting and re-centering continues as your breathing slows further and you continue to relax.

After a while, tell yourself that because of what you are doing or just did, you are now ready to just drift off into sleep.
Feel that with each breath, you are becoming more tired and sinking further into the bed.

Music Starts and Stops

After performing both relaxation routines:
Keep your eyes closed, tell yourself that what you are about to do is going to help you get ready to sleep. Take three further long deep breaths, as you try to feel yourself sinking into the bed.

Then, imagine you are sitting in a comfortable chair in a cozy bedroom. There is a CD player and you can just make out the sound of some light violin music; almost too quiet to hear. You continue to listen to the faint music as you breathe deeply.

After three long deep breaths you notice that the music has stopped. But then after three more deep breaths the music starts again, very quietly as before. This pattern repeats and continues.

After a while, tell yourself that because of what you are doing or just did, you are now ready to just drift off into sleep. Feel that with each breath, you are becoming more tired and sinking further into the bed.

Icy Table

After performing both relaxation routines:
Keep your eyes closed, tell yourself that what you are about to do is going to help you get ready to sleep. Take three further long deep breaths, as you try to feel yourself sinking into the bed.

Then, see yourself sitting at a table. The table top has ice across it and in the middle of the table is an upturned glass inside a circle marked on the ice. The table slowly tilts in one direction meaning the glass slides out of place. You stop the glass from moving and return it to the middle of the table. As you do this the table top levels out again.

After three long deep breaths, the table tilts again slightly in a different direction. Again, imagine you reach out and stop the glass from moving, returning it to the center as the table levels out once more. This pattern continues, after every three breaths.

After a while, tell yourself that because of what you are doing or just did, you are now ready to just drift off into sleep.
Feel that with each breath, you are becoming more tired and sinking further into the bed.

Snowy Hill

After performing both relaxation routines:
Keep your eyes closed, tell yourself that what you are about to do is going to help you get ready to sleep. Take three further long deep breaths, as you try to feel yourself sinking into the bed.

Then, see yourself next to a sled at the top of a snowy hill on a bright sunny day. You get into the sled and start sliding down the hill. After three more long deep breaths you notice the hill suddenly levels out and the sled slows down but doesn't stop. You continue to breathe deeply.

Imagine the sled then comes to another down slope, and again you slide down. After three more long deep breaths you find the hill levels out and you slow down once again. This pattern repeats every three breaths.

After a while, tell yourself that because of what you are doing or just did, you are now ready to just drift off into sleep. Feel that with each breath, you are becoming more tired and sinking further into the bed.

Watch the Birdie

After performing both relaxation routines:
Keep your eyes closed, tell yourself that what you are about to do is going to help you get ready to sleep. Take three further long deep breaths, as you try to feel yourself sinking into the bed.

Then, imagine you are sitting at the top of a small hill enjoying the lovely countryside all around you. You can feel a gentle breeze on your face when you look out and see a bird flying across in front of you. The bird flies around the hill and then appears back in front of you again.

This happens after every two long, deep breaths that you take. You begin to count how many times you see the bird. After a while it seems the bird becomes tired and it now appears after every *four* long deep breaths; this continues.

After a while, tell yourself that because of what you are doing or just did, you are now ready to just drift off into sleep.
Feel that with each breath, you are becoming more tired and sinking further into the bed.

Long Run

After performing both relaxation routines:
Keep your eyes closed, tell yourself that what you are about to do is going to help you get ready to sleep. Take three further long deep breaths, as you try to feel yourself sinking into the bed.

Then, imagine that you just got back from a long run. After a shower you see yourself sitting in an armchair and relaxing. You start to think about how tiring the run was, your legs feel very heavy and you are so pleased the run is over.

As you do this you take five more long, deep breaths, enjoying the sensation of feeling fully relaxed sitting in the comfortable chair. Begin to count your breaths in sets of three, as you become more and more relaxed and your breathing slows further.

After a while, tell yourself that because of what you are doing or just did, you are now ready to just drift off into sleep.
Feel that with each breath, you are becoming more tired and sinking further into the bed.

Colored Cars

After performing both relaxation routines:
Keep your eyes closed, tell yourself that what you are about to do is going to help you get ready to sleep. Take three further long deep breaths, as you try to feel yourself sinking into the bed.

Then, imagine you are sitting in a car factory, looking down on the production line from an office on the third floor. You are bored, and decide to start to watch the cars as they roll off the production line. You continue to breathe deeply, and notice that after every third breath another car leaves the line, and is driven away.

You also notice that each car is a different color. *You* decide the color in question and say it to yourself as the car rolls off. This continues, yet becomes more difficult, as you begin to feel increasingly tired.

After a while, tell yourself that because of what you are doing or just did, you are now ready to just drift off into sleep. Feel that with each breath, you are becoming more tired and sinking further into the bed.

Bus in Motion

After performing both relaxation routines:
Keep your eyes closed, tell yourself that what you are about to do is going to help you get ready to sleep. Take three further long deep breaths, as you try to feel yourself sinking into the bed.

Then, imagine you're sitting on a bus that is going on a journey through country lanes. Your eyes are closed yet you can sense the motion of the bus either right or left as it follows the road.

You notice that the motion seems to occur in time with your breathing. After two long, deep breaths, you feel your weight move very slightly to the right.

After two further long deep breaths, your weight moves slightly to the left. This continues as the bus continues its journey, you relax further enjoying the motion of the bus.

After a while, tell yourself that because of what you are doing or just did, you are now ready to just drift off into sleep. Feel that with each breath, you are becoming more tired and sinking further into the bed.

Spell It Out

After performing both relaxation routines:
Keep your eyes closed, tell yourself that what you are about to do is going to help you get ready to sleep. Take three further long deep breaths, as you try to feel yourself sinking into the bed.

Then, slowly begin to think about the word sleep. Think about each letter of the word in turn as follows: After a long deep breath visualize the letter 's' while thinking about the sound of the letter. After two further deep breaths repeat for the letter 'l'.

Continue this for the remaining three letters, again with two long deep breaths between each letter. Once you have completed this for all the letters, visualize and think about the word sleep again.

Repeat this again, visualizing the word and each of the letters, taking two long deep breaths between each; continue this as long as you can.

After a while, tell yourself that because of what you are doing or just did, you are now ready to just drift off into sleep. Feel that with each breath, you are becoming more tired and sinking further into the bed.

Deeper.. Deeper

After performing both relaxation routines:
Keep your eyes closed, tell yourself that what you are about to do is going to help you get ready to sleep. Take three further long deep breaths, as you try to feel yourself sinking into the bed.

Then, think about trying to increase the delay between each breath, telling yourself that by doing this it will make it easier for you to fall asleep. Begin to count to three between each breath, and focus on controlling the beginning and end of each breath.

This deeper and more balanced breathing pattern will help you further relax and clear your mind. Feel yourself sinking down deeper into the bed, as your breathing continues to slow.

After a while, tell yourself that because of what you are doing or just did, you are now ready to just drift off into sleep. Feel that with each breath, you are becoming more tired and sinking further into the bed.

Folding Paper

After performing both relaxation routines:
Keep your eyes closed, tell yourself that what you are about to do is going to help you get ready to sleep. Take three further long deep breaths, as you try to feel yourself sinking into the bed.

Then, imagine you are sitting at a table with a square piece of white paper in front of you. You have been told by a friend that imagining you are calmly folding the paper should help you to fall asleep. So you want to get started, but take a couple more long deep breaths first. You then make the first fold of the paper diagonally, so you have formed a triangle. As you look down at the triangle, take three long deep breaths, before folding the paper again in half to form a smaller triangle.

Take three further deep breaths, and then fold the paper one last time so you have an even smaller triangle. Then imagine you put this to one side before repeating the process with a fresh piece of paper. Continue the three breath pattern between folds, and continue with further sheets of paper as necessary.

After a while, tell yourself that because of what you are doing or just did, you are now ready to just drift off into sleep.
Feel that with each breath, you are becoming more tired and sinking further into the bed.

Pencil Circles

After performing both relaxation routines:
Keep your eyes closed, tell yourself that what you are about to do is going to help you get ready to sleep. Take three further long deep breaths, as you try to feel yourself sinking into the bed.

Then, imagine you are using a pencil to slowly draw a circle on a sketch pad. You are trying to draw the best circle you can, bearing in mind its freehand. You control the pencil's movement on the paper, and also control your breathing.

Try to finish the circle in the time it takes to breathe long and deep eight times. So each quarter of the circle would be drawn after every two breaths. Once you have finished the circle, begin to draw another circle just inside the first.

Use the same deep breathing pattern as you imagine doing this. Continue to draw a new circle just inside the previous one.

After a while, tell yourself that because of what you are doing or just did, you are now ready to just drift off into sleep. Feel that with each breath, you are becoming more tired and sinking further into the bed.

All Fingers and Thumbs

After performing both relaxation routines:
Keep your eyes closed, tell yourself that what you are about to do is going to help you get ready to sleep. Take three further long deep breaths, as you try to feel yourself sinking into the bed.

Then, steeple the fingers and thumbs on each hand together and hold them there. Next, separate the two thumbs, and hold them apart. Take another long, deep breath then touch the thumbs back together. After a further deep breath, this time separate the index fingers, and hold them apart.

After another deep breath, touch and hold them together again. Continue this for the remaining fingers; again taking a long, deep breath after each separation and rejoining of the fingers together. Once you have done this for all fingers, separate your hands, fully extend the fingers, before clenching your fists. Repeat this three times, before performing the steepling and breathing process again. Repeat and continue, as your breathing slows further. When you feel ready, stop the exercise.

After a while, tell yourself that because of what you are doing or just did, you are now ready to just drift off into sleep. Feel that with each breath, you are becoming more tired and sinking further into the bed.

Platforms and Ladders

After performing both relaxation routines:
Keep your eyes closed, tell yourself that what you are about to do is going to help you get ready to sleep. Take three further long deep breaths, as you try to feel yourself sinking into the bed.

Then, imagine you are standing in front of a strange ladder with sixty rungs along its length. The ladder leads up to a high platform. You hold the ladder, then step up on to the first rung, after you do this you take two long, deep breaths. *The ladder is strange* in that for each rung you climb, the ladder will add nine more to it. So after the first step up, you are ten rungs off the ground.

You then step up on the next rung of the ladder, before taking another two long, deep breaths. Do this six times in total until you reach the platform, following the breathing pattern as you go. See yourself taking a lie down a comfortable bed that is up there. After resting for a while, you find you are back at the foot of the ladder again!

Time to repeat your climb, following the same breathing pattern, until you are back up to the platform, and can again rest for a while. Continue and repeat as your breathing slows further.

After a while, tell yourself that because of what you are doing or just did, you are now ready to just drift off into sleep.
Feel that with each breath, you are becoming more tired and sinking further into the bed.

Bright Lights and Shades

After performing both relaxation routines:
Keep your eyes closed, tell yourself that what you are about to do is going to help you get ready to sleep. Take three further long deep breaths, as you try to feel yourself sinking into the bed.

Then, imagine it is dark and you are lying in a bed next to a very large window. From across the street bright neon light is shining into the room, this is keeping you awake. You are going to pull the shade down over the window to shut out the light. The trouble is the cord is very weak so you can't pull the shade all the way down at once.

Instead you need to pull the cord six separate times, in order to fully lower the blind over the window. After you slowly make the first pull of the cord, take a long deep breath. Then pull the cord again, once more breathing deeply afterwards. Repeat this six times, along with the breathing pattern described.

Once the shade is fully lowered, repeat the process again, while following the same breathing pattern; this continues.

After a while, tell yourself that because of what you are doing or just did, you are now ready to just drift off into sleep.
Feel that with each breath, you are becoming more tired and sinking further into the bed.

Light Sleep

After performing both relaxation routines:
Keep your eyes closed, tell yourself that what you are about to do is going to help you get ready to sleep. Take three further long deep breaths, as you try to feel yourself sinking into the bed.

Then, imagine you are staring at the word 'sleep' on a wall in front of you. The word is in big letters, each of which is illuminated by two bright white LED lights. Your job is to remove the two lights in each of the letters. Beginning with the letter 's' slowly unscrew the first LED light, then after taking a long, deep breath, unscrew the second light.

Next, do the same with the two lights in the second, and remaining three letters, while following the breathing pattern described. Once you have finished with the final letter, 'p', repeat the process and breathing pattern again.

After a while, tell yourself that because of what you are doing or just did, you are now ready to just drift off into sleep.
Feel that with each breath, you are becoming more tired and sinking further into the bed.

Cloud Jumping

After performing both relaxation routines:
Keep your eyes closed, tell yourself that what you are about to do is going to help you get ready to sleep. Take three further long deep breaths, as you try to feel yourself sinking into the bed.

Then, imagine you have jumped out of a plane wearing a parachute. You are high above the clouds; floating down you steer the parachute directly for one of the clouds. To your surprise you find that when you reach the cloud, rather than descending through it.. you can stand on its fluffy top.

You stay there for the time it takes to take two long deep breaths and then jump off the cloud and continue downwards. Soon you see another cloud and again land on its fluffy top.. you again stay for the time it takes to take two long deep breaths as before, and then again jump off and continue downwards.

This repeats until you reach cloud six or seven, at which point, you lie down and rest. You begin to jump down on to the next sequence of clouds, before resting again after the sixth or seventh cloud. This continues.

After a while, tell yourself that because of what you are doing or just did, you are now ready to just drift off into sleep.
Feel that with each breath, you are becoming more tired and sinking further into the bed.

Tumbling Jeans

After performing both relaxation routines:
Keep your eyes closed, tell yourself that what you are about to do is going to help you get ready to sleep. Take three further long deep breaths, as you try to feel yourself sinking into the bed.

Then, imagine you are in front of a tumble dryer that is turning very slowly. As you look through the glass at the drum turning you notice that there seems to be just a pair of blue jeans in the machine. As they dry, the jeans are being lifted before then dropping back to the bottom of the drum.

You take a long deep breath and notice that the jeans fall back to the bottom of the drum exactly in time with the breath you just took. You watch this for a while, seeing the drying jeans drop back to the bottom of the drum, after every full breath you take and become comfortable with this pattern.

You stare at the drum window, allowing yourself to become more and more relaxed as the jeans continue to tumble in time with your breathing.

After a while, tell yourself that because of what you are doing or just did, you are now ready to just drift off into sleep.
Feel that with each breath, you are becoming more tired and sinking further into the bed.

Bowled Over

After performing both relaxation routines:
Keep your eyes closed, tell yourself that what you are about to do is going to help you get ready to sleep. Take three further long deep breaths, as you try to feel yourself sinking into the bed.

Then, see yourself lying comfortably on a bed, surrounded by six, four foot tall cardboard bowling pins standing upright in front of you. Your task is to knock down the bowling pins, one at a time, by throwing soft bowling ball cushions at them. You'll do this while taking two long deep breaths between each throw.

Imagine the cushions are all around you on the bed. You pick up a cushion, throw it and knock over the first bowling pin. After two long deep breaths you repeat this for the second bowling pin and so on until all the pins have been knocked down.

Then as if by magic, the bowling pins spring back up again in front of you. So, with two deep breaths between each throw you repeat the process again; this continues.

After a while, tell yourself that because of what you are doing or just did, you are now ready to just drift off into sleep.
Feel that with each breath, you are becoming more tired and sinking further into the bed.

Stay On Course

After performing both relaxation routines:
Keep your eyes closed, tell yourself that what you are about to do is going to help you get ready to sleep. Take three further long deep breaths, as you try to feel yourself sinking into the bed.

Then, imagine you are at the helm of a small boat. You are holding the wheel as you move slowly through the waves. It is dark outside and you are heading towards distant lights on a small island.

The current is quite strong however, and you must continue to turn the wheel to the left and then a little later, to the right in order to stay on course for the island. As you slowly turn the wheel left, take a long deep breath. Then, after three more deep breaths, see yourself turning the wheel to the right.

After three further deep breaths, again turn the wheel slowly to the left. Continue this process of turning the wheel, to the left and right, while following the deep breathing pattern described.

Every so often, you find your head drops because you are growing increasingly tired. Despite this, you are confident that you will eventually reach the island.

After a while, tell yourself that because of what you are doing or just did, you are now ready to just drift off into sleep. Feel that with each breath, you are becoming more tired and sinking further into the bed.

Calmer View

After performing both relaxation routines:
Keep your eyes closed, tell yourself that what you are about to do is going to help you get ready to sleep. Take three further long deep breaths, as you try to feel yourself sinking into the bed.

Then, as your eyes settle behind the eyelids you become aware of dull flashes and shades of dark and light. In order to more easily drift off to sleep, gradually try to see these bolder brighter shades slowly *dissolve* into smaller particles that are more evenly spread.

As you try to concentrate on this, continue to breathe deeply. Try to be content with a very slow reduction in the number of flashes, or bigger shades of dark and light as they give way to a calmer less active view. Think about this as your breathing continues to slow.

After a while, tell yourself that because of what you are doing or just did, you are now ready to just drift off into sleep.
Feel that with each breath, you are becoming more tired and sinking further into the bed.

Polished to a Shine

After performing both relaxation routines:
Keep your eyes closed, tell yourself that what you are about to do is going to help you get ready to sleep. Take three further long deep breaths, as you try to feel yourself sinking into the bed.

Then, imagine you are sitting down holding a bowling ball in your lap. The ball is covered in marks and smudges and you are going to polish it until it is shiny once again. Using a small soft towel you begin to work around the ball with both hands as you polish it and remove the marks.

After three or four deep breaths, adjust the ball in your lap so that you can continue to slowly polish it with both hands. Every three or four breaths adjust the ball again so you can continue to slowly polish it. Keep polishing and breathing deeply until you feel the ball is shiny enough and the marks have all been removed. Repeat and continue this process with further balls.

After a while, tell yourself that because of what you are doing or just did, you are now ready to just drift off into sleep. Feel that with each breath, you are becoming more tired and sinking further into the bed.

Blowing in the Wind

After performing both relaxation routines:
Keep your eyes closed, tell yourself that what you are about to do is going to help you get ready to sleep. Take three further long deep breaths, as you try to feel yourself sinking into the bed.

Then, imagine you are lying in bed, in the dark, next to an open window. The corner of the drape covering the window flaps every so often as the wind outside gently blows against it. Every time this happens, moonlight shines in under the drape. It's relaxing to watch this and your breathing slows as you do so.

You notice that the drape begins to flap regularly, seemingly following your breathing pattern. Every three breaths, the drape flaps again. After a while, you begin to feel more tired and notice that the drape begins to flap less often, eventually stopping as the wind dies down.

After a while, tell yourself that because of what you are doing or just did, you are now ready to just drift off into sleep.
Feel that with each breath, you are becoming more tired and sinking further into the bed.

Other Considerations for Better Sleep

Other commonly shared considerations for improved sleep include:

- Avoid too much nicotine, caffeine and alcohol generally, but especially close to bedtime.
- Try to avoid eating, especially large meals, late in the evening.
- Try to go to bed at, and wake up at, the same time each day.
- Avoid lengthy use of light emitting screens, just before bedtime.
- Ensure your sleeping environment is free of any noise and also sufficiently dark.
- Try to ensure you make time for regular physical activity during your day.
- Avoid long daytime naps if possible.
- Keep the time you allow for sleep to between seven and nine hours.

About the Author

A.C French lives on Jeju Island, off the coast of South Korea. In his late fifties, married and joint custodian of the second love of his life: a Chipin named Minnie.

In place of any professional qualifications relating to sleep improvement, or sleep disorders is a mind continually looking to solve problems; especially when the problems concerned are known to impact those he loves.

Aside from writing, in his free time, he can be found cycling around the Island and also developing disruptive ideas that he believes will make the world a better place.

Other publications by the author

Cognitive Health of an Elderly Parent
Choux Haiku
The Power of Umm

Contact email address: contactacfrench @gmail.com

Useful Sources of Information

Cleveland Clinic
http://my.clevelandclinic.org/health/diseases/12119-insomnia

Mayo Clinic
https://www.mayoclinic.org/diseases-conditions/insomnia/symptoms-causes/syc-20355167

Web MD
https://www.webmd.com/sleep-disorders/insomnia-symptoms-and-causes

National Institute of Health
https://pmc.ncbi.nlm.nih.gov/articles/PMC1978319/

Health Direct
https://www.healthdirect.gov.au/insomnia

Sleep Foundation
https://www.sleepfoundation.org/insomnia